HMONG MILESTONES IN AMERICA

Citizens in a New World

By Susan Omoto

John Gordon Burke Publisher, Inc.

To Know the Land

Library of Congress Cataloging-in-Publication Data

Omoto, Susan, 1955-
Hmong milestones in America : citizens in a new world / by Susan Omoto.
  p. cm.– (To know the land)
Includes bibliographical references and index.
Contents: Hmong history – Life in Laos – Celebration –The war years – Leaving Laos for Thailand – Life in the camps – Dr. Xoua Thao, first Hmong medical doctor – Ying Vang, first Hmong Catholic priest in the United States – Choua Lee, first elected Hmong official in the United States – – Rev. Bea Vue-Benson, first Hmong woman Lutheran minister – Christopher Thao, first Hmong attorney in the United States – Afterword: bridging two worlds – Hmong glossary.
ISBN 0-934272-56-5 (pbk. : alk. paper) – ISBN 0-934272-57-3 (clothbound)
1. Hmong Americans–History. 2. Hmong Americans–Biography. [1. Hmong Americans.] I. Title. II. Series.

E184.H55 O46 2002
973'.0495942–dc21   2002010431

Credits: Cover Design and Portraits: Ed French.

TABLE OF CONTENTS

INTRODUCTION

The story of what happened to the Hmong as a result of the Vietnam war can be described as a nightmare. It would be difficult to imagine the horrors these mountain-dwelling farmers endured to save their families' lives when the communist Pathet Lao took over their homeland in Laos.

The Hmong lived through years of devastation, watching as entire villages were wiped out by bombs. They witnessed people blown to bits by land mines. And, when it was over, they had to live like fugitives in the jungle where they ran for refuge.

The individual stories of the Hmong exodus from war-torn Laos into Thailand are similar. Some families lived in caves, some covered themselves with banana leaves for shelter at night. No one could stay in one place for very long, for fear they would be caught by the communists. Those that were captured were either killed or sent to "re-education camps" (a code word for concentration camps) where they were worked or starved to death.

The journey of escape to the Mekong River, which runs between Laos and Thailand, was perilous. Many babies died along the way as a result of being over-drugged with opium. It was necessary to keep them from crying so that the soldiers, who were hunting them down, couldn't tell where they were. Many of the Hmong interviewed for this book can remember walking past dead and decaying bodies along the way.

Food was scarce: Some families ate bugs, tree bark, roots, and some even ate their clothes. Occasionally, fleeing families would see orphaned children along the way, eating dirt and rocks. Fires were out of the question because the smoke would give away the family's location. Travel was done in complete silence.

People who finally made it to the river had to find a way to cross into Thailand, where refugee camps were waiting. Most Hmong couldn't swim such a long distance, so they tied together bamboo and used it as a raft. Some filled plastic bags with air and tucked them under their arms. Sometimes, during the later years of the migration into Thailand, border patrols would shoot people in the river. Many refugees' bodies lie at the bottom of the Mekong River.

Once the Hmong reached refugee camps in Thailand, they were forced to live in filth, dirt, and extremely crowded conditions. There was no privacy. There was no way for them to live a normal life. Some of the luckier people had small garden plots and kept busy growing what little food they could. Despair set in for some, who committed suicide. They were either hopeless about getting out of the camps or not able to live with the horror they had seen along the way. Self-sufficiency was a point of pride for the Hmong, but the war took that pride away by making them dependent on others for survival.

The year 2001 marked a quarter-century since the first Hmong refugees arrived in the United States from camps in Thailand. The distance these primitive farmers traveled cannot be measured merely in miles; it is more like moving through two hundred years in the time span of a long airplane ride.

Laos and the United States are as far apart in miles as they are in climate, social structure, and communication. However, many Hmong overcame these obstacles and made great strides personally and professionally once they reached the United States. This book tells a few of their inspiring stories. They are stories of stark contrasts: the Hmong life in Laos and the Hmong life in the United States.

Unlike previous immigrants to the United States who had some exposure to Western culture, most Hmong arrived in a totally alien world and attempted to fit in. From that perspective, it is difficult to find a group of more disadvantaged immigrants than the Hmong refugees who arrived in the United States in 1975.

For one thing, most previous refugees had the advantage of a written language. This made resettlement easier. Relocation agencies in the United States were able to translate important information into material that could be read by each new ethnic group.

It wasn't until the 1950s that missionaries reintroduced a written language to the Hmong. But since education was for the privileged, not very many Hmong arriving in the United States could read. The few who had attended Laos-sponsored schools were taught to read Lao, which is very different from Hmong. It is estimated that Laos has an illiteracy rate of 99%. For all of these reasons, communication between the Hmong and their new world was difficult.

The Hmong are in America because they fought on the side of the United States during the Vietnamese War in Southeast Asia. The Central Intelligence Agency began recruiting Hmong men to fight communists in Laos in the early 1960s for the "secret war" against the North Vietnamese. Most Hmong became soldiers out of financial necessity. They could no longer farm because the war kept them on the move. Some became soldiers because they were forced to do so. As far as the United States was concerned, no one could navigate mountainous regions like the Hmong, and no one could fight as fiercely as the Hmong.

After the war ended, the United States began evacuating Hmong soldiers and their families to the United States. This action was part of a commitment to care for the Hmong in the event that the United States lost the war. Critics of the relocation effort say the United States did a poor job of preparing for the Hmong immigrants by not providing them with adequate housing, job training, English lessons and other basic survival skills.

With the exception of some high-ranking military officers, very few Hmong who arrived in the United States were ready for the differences that were found in culture, social structure, climate, customs and modern conveniences. Many things the Hmong took for granted and held sacred in Laos were illegal in their new country. Traditional Hmong marriages took place around the age of fourteen. In the United States it is usually not legal for a person's sons younger than sixteen to marry. In Laos, hunting, fishing and farming were done whenever and wherever space was available. In American cities, you must hold licenses, observe "no trespassing" signs and pay attention to seasons, game limits, and pollution warnings.

The mountainous areas in Laos had a tropical climate. But refugees arrived in places that had snow on the ground and freezing temperatures—a far cry from the jungles they were used to. Modern conveniences were a mystery to most Hmong, who had never ever seen a toilet, window glass, food in jars or electric lights.

Family clan systems created a structure for Hmong social life in Laos. Crimes and other social issues were resolved by the tribe. Illness was treated by shamans, who were a combination of medicine men and spiritual leaders. There were no medical doctors, no clinics, and no hospitals. The average Hmong life span in Laos was about 46 years.

Perhaps the greatest insult of all came when Americans expressed racial hatred toward Hmong. The irony is that the Hmong never wanted to be in the United States. Misconceptions caused great damage to the Hmong when they first arrived. Many Americans referred to the Hmong as "boat people" when, in fact, the real boat people were Vietnamese. The Hmong were confused with Vietnamese people when, in fact, the Hmong had fought for the United States, not against it. The Hmong expected that the Americans would be grateful for their war efforts. Americans expected the Hmong to be grateful for welfare,

One Hmong man who was interviewed for this book pointed out that racial hatred he encountered was something no one had anticipated. He said the Hmong didn't understand why Americans would yell at them to "go back where they came from." "We didn't want to be here in the first place," he said. "If it wasn't for the fact the communists who had won the war began to kill my people, we would have stayed in Laos. We didn't want to be taken from our country." He went on to explain that no one prepared them for Americans thinking it was a bad thing to receive welfare money. He was told by authorities it was payment for the work they had done during the Vietnamese War. Americans saw it as a free ride.

In this book you will meet some remarkable people. They are Choua Lee, the first Hmong elected to public office in the United States; Christopher Thao, the first Hmong attorney in the United States; Ying Vang, the first Hmong to be ordained a Roman Catholic priest in the United States; Dr. Xoua Thao, the first Hmong to get a medical degree in the United States and Bea Vue-Benson, the first Hmong woman to become an ordained Lutheran minister in the United States.

Each of these pioneers barely escaped their homeland alive. They began a new life in a place where they didn't speak the language, couldn't find their way around, or understand what modern conveniences this new home had in store. It would be difficult not to be impressed by their accomplishments.

CHAPTER 1: HMONG HISTORY

There is a lot of debate as to what the word Hmong means. It really is just a name for a people like the word "Indian" or "American" and doesn't in itself have any particular meaning. Somehow, over the years, though, it has come to mean "free people."—Sucheng Chan, author of "Hmong Means Free."

Oppression and persecution have ruled the lives of the Hmong as far back as anyone can remember. Perhaps best described as a "portable culture," the Hmong were always ready to fight or flee. Their houses were lashed together in sections that could be moved easily. They used embroidered quilts, music and storytelling to keep customs alive. When they traveled, they brought along replaceable items such as knives, baskets and clothing.

The Hmong living in the United States came from Laos, a landlocked country in Southeast Asia. High mountains run between Laos and its northern neighbors, Burma and China. Vietnam is located to the east of Laos, Cambodia to the south and Thailand to the west.

It is not certain where Hmong people originated. Some historians say there is evidence that the Hmong came from Siberia. Others have made connections between the Hmong and Mesopotamia through Hmong legends about the beginning of the world.

Most anthropologists who study the origins of mankind trace the Hmong to China about 5,000 years ago. It is believed that the Hmong settled along the Yellow River and eventually moved to the mountains of China. One thing is certain: the Hmong have been persecuted from the beginning and migration, or moving, has been a central part of their existence.

It is said that the Chinese called the Hmong "Miao" or "Meo," which means barbarians or savages. Many Hmong were used as slaves by the Chinese because of their perceived low status. They were expected to honor the Chinese at all times.

Needless to say, the two groups were not on good terms, so the Hmong kept to themselves in every way.

They wore their own tribal clothing, married within Hmong groups, played their own musical instruments and practiced their own religion. They never used chopsticks like other Asian cultures.

In the sixteenth century, in order to contain and control the Hmong, the Chinese constructed a Hmong Wall which was a smaller version of the Great Wall of China. It was 100 miles long and 10 feet tall. The Hmong had an ancient written language which the Chinese forbade them to read or write. It wasn't until the 1950s that missionaries reintroduced a written language to the Hmong.

At the beginning of the nineteenth century, the Hmong moved to Laos when their king was murdered by the Chinese. Although the majority of Hmong stayed behind, about a half-million migrated to Indochina. They traveled on foot, carrying everything they owned. Little did they know that their migration would be repeated again in the 1970s.

When the Hmong arrived from China, they were again regarded as intruders. This time, they were despised because of their religion. They were animists—people who believe that things like animals, people, trees, and rocks have souls. The Lao were Buddhists, not animists. To avoid conflict, the Hmong moved to the mountains and created a peaceful existence, raising livestock and crops to feed their families. They thrived there until the Vietnam war interrupted their lives.

More than 60 ethnic groups speak several different languages in Laos. The dominant political and cultural group, the Lao, belong to the Tai-speaking people called the Lao Loum (Lao of the lowlands). They grow rice in the wet paddies along the Mekong River valley for a dietary staple and sugar cane and tropical fruits for trade.

In the highlands, the Lao Theung (Lao of the mountain slopes) speak non-Khmer languages and occupy the lower mountain regions, while the Lao Soung (Lao of the mountain tops) speak Tibet-Burmese languages and live at elevations above 3,000 feet. The Hmong belong to this latter group. The mountains are 6,000 to 9,000 feet high, which is about half the height of Mt. McKinley, the highest point in North America.

At the time the Hmong settled in Laos, a young colonial United States was struggling with its own ethnic and race issues. Massachusetts declared marriage between African Americans and whites to be illegal in 1705. The Tuscarora Indian War broke out between Native Americans and the settlers in North Carolina in 1711. The first group of black slaves was brought to the Louisiana Territories in 1716. The French and Indian War began in 1754, with George Washington leading the colonists.

More than two centuries later, the way the Hmong organized their communities paid off, as Laos was drawn into the Vietnamese War. Village life, which had remained virtually unchanged from generation to generation, fostered strong family ties. If it weren't for strong family ties the Hmong forged over the centuries, survival through the upheaval which resulted from the Vietnamese War would have been nearly impossible.

CHAPTER 2: LIFE IN LAOS

I am not sure of the exact year of my birth because we don't have a writing system and Mom and Dad don't read or write. Mom said I was born when the rice stalks were about this high above the ground (two feet above the ground). We figured it must be around May or June so we put my birthday on June 2.—Dr. Xoua Thao.

Most American children are born in hospitals. Most are not forced to move every six months to keep ahead of bombs dropping on their houses. Most kids grow up with a television, refrigerator and toilet in their homes.

If there weren't highways where they live, there certainly are roads. When American children lie in bed they probably look up at a plaster ceiling instead of a thatched roof made of palm leaves harvested from a nearby jungle.

Hmong houses were usually rectangular and built on the ground, with dirt floors which were swept clean each day. The two entrances of the house faced south and north. There usually weren't any windows. The house had to be large, since it was customary for several generations to live under one roof.

When the Hmong began to move to keep ahead of the war, they usually didn't even bother with huts. If they made it halfway to where they were going and had to stay the night, they would cut bamboo, make a tiny house to protect themselves and then move on in the morning. In some cases, caves served as temporary housing while they hid.

Under normal circumstances, villages would have to move every ten years or so to take advantage of new land for farming. The Hmong are called migratory because they don't have permanent homes, moving from place to place over the course of time, in search of new farmland and other sources of food.

A traditional Hmong village was occupied by groups that varied in size from as few as 100 to as many as 500. The Hmong lifestyle was organized around an economic system based on agriculture, a belief system based on ancestor worship and a social structure based on kinship ties to the father's family, known as a clan system.

The clan or *xeem* system is a social structure based on last names. There are eighteen clans. If there is someone with the same last name in another village, a Hmong person will consider them to be a clan member and will welcome them as family.

The older people of the village, the elders, are in charge of keeping the village organized and running smoothly. If a crime were committed, the issue would be taken up with the elders. They would listen to both sides of the dispute and decide what to do. If a person was guilty as charged, they would have to either drink sacred water which would presumably kill him if he was lying, or they would pay restitution in money or chickens or would wash the victim's face and ask forgiveness. Everything was resolved on the spot by the elders.

Everyone looked out for each other. For instance, if a woman lost her husband to death, she would marry the youngest brother of her husband's family. That was his obligation. This was how men ended up with more than one wife. If a man were already married, he would still have to marry the widow. If he wasn't already married and the relationship didn't work out, he could take another bride.

When it came time to move the family to avoid being bombed in the war, a new home was built out of material found in the jungles. They didn't hire contractors and they didn't rent a U-Haul. They arrived at their new destinations on foot, carrying or dragging all that they owned with them.

The Hmong used "slash-and-burn" farming, which is done by clearing trees and underbrush and then burning the vegetation. The ashes made the soil fertile for farming. The family could farm that land for about four or five years, until the soil would be used up. The monsoons that came each year usually washed away nutrients in the soil. After about four years, it was time to find another area to farm, usually within walking distance.

Farming was hard work. There were no tractors to

work the soil. Everything was done by hand. Hmong farmers used oxen to help clear the land and plow the fields. They would plant seeds by poking a stick in the ground to make a hole and then drop the seeds into the hole. The process was always the same: the first hole was dug and planted for the birds; the second hole was planted for the squirrels and the third hole was planted for the dead. The rest of the crop was for the farmer.

Hmong farmers grew enough crops to feed their families, plus a little extra to use in trade for cloth or pans or other household items. Historically, the only cash crop they grew was the drug opium. In the 1950s, the French bought opium from the Hmong, but when the communists took over the Hmong lost that market and opium was grown only for medicinal use.

A typical farmer's livestock could include oxen, pigs, chickens and maybe some goats. There were dogs and cats, but not kept as pets as they are in America. They congregated around the villages just like squirrels and birds do in America.

Hmong villages and farms had no electricity. When night fell, it was time to go to sleep. If they needed light, they burned oil lamps. Brothers and sisters slept together on bamboo beds or *txaj* in one room and parents slept in another partitioned area, which ran along one wall of the hut. The children slept separated from the parents, unless they were babies or very young.

The villages didn't have running water or flush toilets. That meant families had to haul water from the streams or dig their own wells. When they had to go to the bathroom, they used the jungle.

There were usually two fireplaces in Hmong homes. One was a big fire pit where the family cooked the meals of rice and vegetables, burned wood or prepared food for the animals. In addition, a small fire could be built in another corner where guests would sit and stories would be told. Without a written language, storytelling played a big role in Hmong communities. Many hours were spent together as the elders recounted history, rituals and legends.

In the morning, families woke up to the crowing of roosters as the sun came up over the mountains. The father and the others who worked on the farm got up first and ate a small breakfast of rice. They left early for the fields so that by noon or early afternoon they would have a lot of work accomplished. If a boy was lucky enough to attend school, he would get up a little later and have breakfast before starting the long trek to school.

Whatever their ages, family members shared duties. The young people usually gathered twigs for the fire and looked for old roots and seeds to feed to the animals.

A typical day, described by an elderly Hmong woman, went like this: In the season when you have to attend to the rice field, you get up at first cock crow. In the other seasons you wake up at second or third cock crow, which is still before dawn. The first thing you do is light the lamp filled with oil and a homemade cloth wick. Then you cook the rice for the children. Then you clean the house with the broom you made yourself from grasses. After you are finished you go and cut wild grass for the pigs and cows. You feed the chickens. Then you walk to the fields which are far away. You carry your babies on your back, but if you have lots of children, you can leave some behind with the older ones. When you get home that night you go to the stream and carry water for cooking and bathing in a barrel on your back. You bathe the babies by boiling the water and pouring it with a smaller bowl. The older ones bathe themselves. You bring corn for the chickens and feed the pigs again and then you cook for your family. You usually eat leftover rice from the first meal with a little vegetable. You only eat meat about once a month. After dinner you sew by the light of the lamp. In the fields you wear clothes that are old and ripped up, but you need the new clothes for the New Year. It is bad luck to wear old clothes then.

CHAPTER 3: CELEBRATIONS

We were hard-working people, but we took time out to celebrate certain things. The biggest celebrations I remember were when a new baby arrived, the New Year, marriage and when someone died. We didn't have annual birthday or anniversary celebrations like we do here [in America].—Dr. Xoua Thao.

Like other semi-nomadic cultures, the Hmong have always placed great emphasis on traditional dress. Their costumes are a special symbol of ethnic pride.

There are categories of costumes that define the various Hmong subgroups. There are the White, Green (Blue), Black and Red Striped and Flowery subgroups throughout Southeast Asia. Each of these groups have some subtle differences of language, much like the different dialects spoken within a geographic region. In the United States, the predominant divisions are the White Hmong or *Hmoob Ntsuab*, and the Green Hmong or *Hmoob Dawb*.

The White Hmong costume is characterized by its finely pleated hemp skirt and elaborate and fine embroidery. The costumes of the Green Hmong feature strong patterns and striking color contrasts. Green Hmong women use batik or wax-resist type of dyed fabric. They do not practice reverse appliqué like their White Hmong relatives.

Hmong girls learn to sew at an early age. The creation of Hmong costumes requires years of training in the techniques of appliqé, embroidery, and batik. They must know how color works together to tell the Hmong stories and they must know Hmong myth and ritual. These colorful costumes are referred to as a flower cloth or *paj ntaub*.

Here is how author Anne Fadiman describes getting dressed in traditional Hmong costume:

"First [came] the *phaum*, a pink and black sash about twenty feet long that was wound around me like a ribbon around a maypole.... Then came the *tiab*, a pink, green, and yellow skirt with about five hundred accordion pleats, which, if it had been spread out, would have been wider than I was tall. Its cross-stiching was so fine it looked like beading. Over that went a pink brocade *sev*, or kind of apron.... On my upper half I wore a blue-and-black jacket called a *tsho* and *hnab tshos*, pocket-like bags decorated with dangling silver coins which were hung bandolier-style across my chest. Around my neck went a five-tier necklace of hollow silver. Around my calves, a pair of black puttees called *nrhoob*. Placed upon my head was a *kausmom*, a pink, green and yellow hat decorated with silver coins which jingled when I moved my head."

The Hmong *paj ntaub* or flower cloth plays a significant role in all Hmong ceremonies, as it symbolizes the beginning and the end of human life. It takes years for Hmong women to create elaborate costumes for their daughters or granddaughters. Traditional dress is worn by the Hmong at New Year celebrations, weddings, birth and as part of the funeral.

BIRTH: Hmong babies were born at home. The mother gave birth while she squatted on the floor and let the babies slip into her arms. Soon after each child's birth, the father would dig a hole at least two feet deep in the dirt floor and bury the afterbirth.

If the baby was a boy, his afterbirth, or placenta, would be buried in a place of honor, near the base of the house's central wooden pillar. This is where the male spirit of the house watched over the family. A girl's placenta would be buried under her parents' bed.

In the Hmong language, the word for placenta, or *tsho*, means "shirt." When a Hmong person dies, his or her soul must travel back to the burial place of its *tsho* and put it on. Only after the soul is properly dressed in the clothes it was born in can it continue the journey to be reunited with its ancestors and eventually come back as the soul of a newborn baby. If the soul cannot find its shirt, it will never be able to settle.

When the first Hmong women gave birth in American hospitals, they were confused when hospital staff took the placenta away. As this is such an important practice for the Hmong, however, many hospitals in the Unites States now allow the parents to take their baby's placenta home with them.

All births were occasions for celebration. Three days after birth, a feast was planned and the entire family was invited to help welcome the new baby into the clan and to name the baby. During the celebration, care was taken not to give the newborn too much attention, for fear the spirits would capture the baby's soul.

The naming ceremony or soul-calling, *Hu Plig*, happened on the third day after a baby's birth. It is said that the families waited to see if the baby would live. Until this ceremony was performed, the baby wasn't considered a member of the human race. If it died during the first three days, it was not given funerary rites. This precaution was thought to be necessary in a place where fifty percent of the babies did not survive.

During the ceremony, the soul-caller would brush the baby's hand with a bundle of white strings that would be symbolic of "sweeping away illness." Then, everyone would take a string and tie it around the baby's wrist, to bind the newborn's soul to its body.

The new baby and its mother would be presented with *paj htaub*, an embroidered baby carrier that was used to strap the baby to the mother's back. The baby also received a simple silver necklace, which warned spirits that he or she belonged to a family.

The baby was also given a hat. The Hmong believe that without protection from a hat, a child's spirit will escape through its head. Tassels, pompons, ribbons and yarn were added to the hat. The idea was to disguise the child's head as a flower so that when bad spirits looked down on a baby's head, they would mistake it for a flower and move on.

THE NEW YEAR: According to Fong Lee, author of "The Traditions of Hmong New Year," the expression, "to eat the feast of the 30th" or *not tsiab pebcaug* is the traditional way to talk about the New Year celebration. That is because the feast of the Hmong New Year starts one day before the New Year. The pig is eaten on the 30th of the 12th lunar month based on how the moon looks from the ground in Laos.

Lee writes that it is now customary for Hmong in the United States to say *nyob zoo xyoo tshiab* which literally translates into "stay put well in the New Year."

New Year's is a celebration to wash away bad fortune and to bless the community with good luck. It was a very special time for the Hmong to celebrate the harvest. Each family would spend the whole year raising a pig called "feast pig" or *tus npua tsiab*. It was slaughtered for the New Year celebration and prepared for ritual.

A family would kill their feast pig, put on their best clothing and celebrate for two weeks. During this period they would "rest" their knives and other tools they used in the fields. Then, in early January, they would start the new slash-and-burn and women would begin a new round of sewing for coming next year.

On New Year's Eve, the Hmong conduct a traditional ritual ceremony called *lwm sub or qaib*. It begins in the afternoon and must take place before other ceremonies. It is a ceremony for washing away the old and bad news and bringing forth the new and good news. Family members walk around a New Year's pole, three times forward and three times backward and a rooster is sacrificed as part of the ritual ceremony. Afterwards, families go to their homes and conduct other ritual ceremonies such as *hu plig*, or the calling of the spirit, and *pe tsiab*, or honoring the elders and ancestors.

A traditional Hmong New Year celebration in Laos has activities such as bullfights, sports competitions and talent shows. The Hmong New Year celebration is also a time for young people to find their mates, as they have been working all year and have not had time for courtship. One of the ways they get to know one another is by playing a ball game called *pov pob*. Boys and girls stand in lines facing each other and toss small fabric balls back and forth.

MARRIAGE: Marriage is a very important goal for most Hmong men and women. Marriage is the way in which clan and lineage are continued, as it is only through marriage that children are produced. One of the principal ways of finding a mate is at the New Year celebration. The New Year's game, *pov pob*, typically provides an outlet for the emergence of more intense romances. A marriage proposal must be made by the man's family, and one important part in the proposal is his promise to love the woman, as evidenced by a willingness to pay a bride price. Marriage in normal circumstances is arranged by *mej koob*, or go-betweens. Two people whom the families respect and who are not from the same clan serve as negotiators between the bride's and groom's families. The negotiation can be very complex. It may last for several days, depending upon the relationship between the two families.

Young people usually get married after the new year, between the first and the fifteenth of the month; Hmong tend not to get married after the month of June. Hmong believe the new year is a good time for marriage, because everything starts new and is accompanied by a new moon. Hmong people often have married at very young ages in the past. Most youth—especially girls—were married by the time they were fifteen years old. In the Hmong culture, it is not permissible to marry a person with the same clan name.

The day of the wedding meant a time for celebration. New clothes and *paj ntaub* that had been made for the bride and groom were worn. Music also played an important role.

During the wedding ceremony and banquet, the souls and good fortune of the young couple were symbolically wrapped up inside an umbrella that was tied with a band that had been wrapped around the turban of the bride. The umbrella was carried in a procession to the groom's house, where another banquet was held. The *Khi Tes* ceremony followed, in which strings were tied around the wrists of the couple and blessings were given to them.

FUNERALS: Death was the most important ritual for the Hmong, since their belief system centers around ancestor worship. An elaborate three-day ceremony takes place, followed by an additional thirteen days of ritual. Then, one year after death, the deceased is again remembered with a ceremony.

Back in Laos, the Hmong have no funeral homes or undertakers. The person who has died is kept inside the house, dressed up and tied onto a stretcher. The person is given gifts that will protect his or her soul from bad spirits during the trip to the ancestral world. A mature rooster is often killed to help guide the deceased's soul.

The musical instrument, called the *qeej*, is played at the funeral. It is a bamboo mouth organ that sounds like someone speaking. During the funeral, the *qeej* plays constantly, aiding the souls of the deceased in their journeys to the grave site and to the realm of the other world. When condensed moisture drips from the holes in the *qeej*, the dead person's spirit sees it as coins dropping from the sky. The Hmong term for the ceremony is *kab ke pam tuag* or "Showing the Way."

It is during the "Showing the Way" ritual that the soul begins its trip by first collecting the placenta. Then it climbs stairs toward heaven for thirteen days, crosses a salty river and a bitter spring before encountering many other supernatural challenges on its way to heaven.

The Hmong value the body in death as much as in life. It is critical that bodies are treated correctly so they can be reincarnated. The deceased is dressed in an elaborate costume with a large collar having a pattern called the dreaming maze stitched upon it.

Hmong are buried with ornamental shoes that are used to walk through the land of the giant furry caterpillars on the way to the other world. The fingers of the dead person often are tied with red threads so that if the person is detained in the afterlife by spirits wanting them to help peel onions and garlic, they can say their fingers are injured and cannot help.

During the funeral ceremony, while the body is in the house, relatives and neighbors come and go. Animals are killed each day, enough to make food for all the visitors. These great feasts not only honor the dead person's spirits and those of his or her ancestors, but also help the traveling spirit along its journey.

In America, Hmong funerals closely follow tradition in order to respect the process of reincarnation. Many Hmong funerals feature feasts and long ceremonies. However, Hmong are buried in caskets, as required by law. Funeral homes will remove all the metal parts of a casket at the request of the Hmong family. It is believed that being buried with any metal interferes with decomposition and, therefore, with reincarnation.

A common practice for Hmong celebrations is the tradition of giving squares of elaborate hand-stitched cloth or *paj ntaub*. When a person accumulates enough squares, they are stitched together on a large piece of fabric with a border of triangles, which is said to scare away evil spirits.

Music, which plays a major role in all Hmong ceremonies, was handed down from generation to generation. Their music, like their flower cloth, is a symbol of life. The sounds are meant to be like human voices.

During the funeral, the *khxa k* or farewell song to the dead may last more than an hour. The song is played with a *qeej* and drum. It is extremely important to follow exact form during performance rituals in order to satisfy the requirements of life and death transitions.

CHAPTER 4: THE WAR YEARS

When people ask me, Xoua, what does it feel like being a refugee?, I have to tell them I was a refugee long before I ever came here to the United States.—Dr. Xoua Thao.

In May, 1975, Saigon and South Vietnam fell to communism, ending America's involvement in the long war in Southeast Asia. The war in Vietnam had more casualties (people killed and injured) than all previous wars combined. During this war, the Hmong fought with U. S. forces against communism.

Even though most people associate the 1960s and 1970s with the Vietnam War, trouble started long before that. Laos was under partial French control for nearly 50 years, beginning in 1887. French interest in the Hmong was limited to the Hmong farming of opium poppies, which the French made into an export business. But during World War II, the Hmong also become useful to the French when Hmong guerrilla soldiers fought the Japanese in the Laotian jungles.

After World War II, the French were involved in a struggle in Southeast Asia to keep communism out of Laos. By 1954, the French withdrew and the United States took over the fight. In an attempt to fight against the Laotian communist faction called the Pathet Lao, the United States organized the Royal Lao Army. By 1959 the United States Central Intelligence Agency (CIA) was recruiting people who lived in the mountains of Laos. These people were the Hmong.

The Hmong fighting force was put under control of the CIA. The agency elevated the only Hmong commissioned officer in the Royal Lao Army, Lt. Col. Vang Pao, to the rank of general and encouraged him to organize eighty-four companies of Hmong infantry, who existed to harass the communists.

Without playing any official role in Laos, the CIA supplied Vang Pao's forces under cover of a government organization that was supposed to help refugees—the United States Agency for Aid and Development.

In retaliation for harassment, the communists dropped bombs with yellow ashes and red ashes on Hmong communities, which made villagers sick with nosebleeds. They would drop an acid-like rain on the people which would eat away at their skin. Hmong soldiers and villagers didn't have a specific name for the substance other than calling it what it was: poison or *tshuaj lom*.

Defoliants also were used in jungles during the war. These were chemicals that killed plants so it would be easier to detect and see people on the ground. The chemicals also destroyed fields and farms, starving the Hmong population.

While the United States was in Southeast Asia, United States forces dropped supplies for fleeing refugees, such as rice, salt, blankets and live pigs. Whole villages moved to areas where they knew there would be rice drops. But, in 1971, the United States Agency for Aid and Development begin reducing air support. In 1974, they declared they would no longer help the refugees.

The war was devastating to the Hmong. By 1971, many Hmong families had no males left over the age of ten, because they had been killed while fighting the communists. Before the war was over, about one-third of the entire Laotian Hmong population was killed.

Since many of the heaviest battles were fought near villages, great numbers of people had to flee. Most families had to leave things behind, such as livestock, household items, crops and other food.

Dr. Xoua Thao remembers the bombings and the relief packages.

"I remember the planes that came in and dropped rice for the people who had to flee. Mom and Dad used to say we had to go close to the village when the rice would be dropped so we could get something for the children. God, it was hard. Sometimes we would want to settle in a certain village but the rice drop was too far away. So on we would go."

Even though United States involvement in Vietnam was widely publicized, its involvement in Laos was kept a secret for many years after the war. Citizens of the United States didn't know about all the promises that had been made to the Hmong, pledging to help them when the war ended. The Hmong were left to fend for themselves in the jungles, afraid they would be killed by the communists, who blamed the Hmong people for preventing their peaceful takeover of Laos.

Some families didn't get out fast enough. They ended up living in caves or in the jungles for months at a time. They lived off the land, eating anything they could find, including insects. But they couldn't stay in one place for much longer than two months or they risked being found by soldiers.

Each day, they would have to venture further away from their homes to gather food. It meant someone could find their trails and follow them home.

During the war, and before they began to leave Laos, Hmong families were never in one place long enough to get settled. It wasn't uncommon for missiles to hit and kill entire families in their homes.

The ground would shake, a bomb would strike and there would be a huge hole left. Everything would be wiped out.

CHAPTER 5: LEAVING LAOS FOR THAILAND

I've heard about families who would start across the river with five or six people tied together, only to find out on the other side they were towing dead family members behind them.—Dr. Xoua Thao.

In 1975, the Pathet Lao won the war. The United States then began to airlift Hmong supporters to Thailand, starting with General Vang Pao and high-ranking Hmong military officers. Hmong who had fought against the communists felt especially vulnerable after the war ended. The Vietnamese suspected all Hmong of collaborating with the United States and every Hmong person believed they were targets for extermination.

Forty thousand refugees headed toward the airlift operation in the city of Long Cheng with their worldly possessions strapped to their backs. Panic spread as Hmong tried to escape their homeland.

They believed that they would be killed by the Pathet Lao for helping the United States if they didn't leave. Those who weren't air lifted out had no choice but to hide in the jungle with their families—some for as long as two years.

For months, a mass exodus out of Laos was taking place. No one knows exactly how many Hmong attempted the trip into Thailand. It is estimated that at least half of them died trying. If disease, snakebite or starvation didn't get them, there was a pretty good chance that the Pathet Lao and Vietnamese bullets would.

The Hmong had been promised by the United States that they would be protected and helped after the war. Because the entire operation in Laos was a secret, however, it took years for the United States to publicly acknowledge its promise. Meanwhile, Hmong refugees were running for their lives to avoid prison camps set up by the new government.

Hmong swam across the Mekong River and slashed through jungles just to get to Thailand and live in relocation camps in hope of being eligible for relocation. The able-bodied carried the elderly, sick, wounded and young.

Some were left to die at the side of the trail. Those who died weren't buried; it was too dangerous to take the time to bury anyone. They were left to rot in the jungle. It was very difficult for them to leave behind the dead. Without proper funeral rites, these souls would be destined to wander forever.

The nomadic Hmong tribe was seeing history repeat itself. It was time to move on, only this time they would have to travel nine thousand miles to start over.

Dr. Xoua Thao's father was willing to take the risk of getting out of Laos in order to give his family a chance for freedom and an opportunity for education. Because he was a part of the secret U.S. Army, he knew what the United States offered his family and he made the decision to go to the refugee camps in Thailand.

"One night, my dad and my oldest brother, who had been a soldier, told us we were going to leave Laos," said Thao. "So we packed up what little we could carry and started off across the jungle. I think we must have walked all night long, carefully stepping in the same footsteps as the person in front of us. If we didn't follow the path exactly we could easily step on a land mine and get blown up."

Thao's family was one of the first groups of refugees to leave Laos. It was a little easier for them than it was for the next wave of refugees. Thao said his father recalled being treated with respect by the Thai but knows of other horrific stories that took place a few years later.

For a short time, refugees were welcome in Thailand, but as more and more people flooded into the country, the Thai became hostile toward them and began demanding money or stealing from them.

Thao tells how some people were robbed and dumped in the middle of the river after their silver was taken. A few years later, the border was patrolled by police and many people were killed while crossing.

"Once the border patrol took over, things turned into a nightmare for the rest of the refugees. You couldn't believe it. The border police were supposed to shoot to kill, so people would have to be completely quiet as they crossed the water," said Thao.

"I've heard about families who would start across the river with five or six people tied together only to find out on the other side some of them were hit by gunfire and killed. They were towing dead family members behind them!" said Thao. "You never knew what was going on when there was so much gunfire."

The Hmong people who crossed the river were so terrified of being shot, they drugged infants with opium to keep them from crying out. They had no choice: If they were to stay in Laos they would be killed by the Pathet Lao.

The Thao family walked from their little village of Pha Lak Pha Kouei to a bus that brought them to the Mekong River, which runs along the border of Laos and Thailand.

"We had some silver bars so we paid them. Five silver bars would take three people across. So it cost us a lot of money and it took us all night to get the entire family across the river into Thailand."

CHAPTER 6: LIFE IN THE CAMPS

There was a lot of death. It was very dirty. There were a lot people with nothing to do all day. The camps were a sharp contrast to the life we were used to living before the war got out of hand.—Dr. Xoua Thao.

There were twenty-one relocation camps set up in Thailand. The Thai didn't fight in the war but they were against communism, and welcomed the Hmong as long as the United States paid for them.

The United States put pressure on the Thai government to set up camps that would accommodate Hmong refugees. The numbers of people were overwhelming and conditions in the camps were horrific. Overcrowding, dirt and disease were rampant. Food was in short supply and malnutrition plagued everyone. Suicide became commonplace as hope ran low.

The median time spent in the camps was five years. Some Hmong refugees decided to pass up the opportunity to move to America because they hoped they would be able to return to Laos. As time went by, most of them eventually realized that was no longer an option.

Some camps were better than others. Chiang Kham had a bad reputation. It had 10-foot bamboo fences surrounding it. Guards were particularly severe and would arrest people for almost anything.

No one was allowed to look outside through the cracks in the bamboo fence. No one was allowed to sell food to the Hmong unless they were approved by the guards, which meant high prices. Refugees were allowed a limited amount of water only at certain times each day. Everyone in the camp was forced to get up early in the morning, stand at attention, salute the Thai flag and sing along as loudspeakers blared the Thai national anthem. If someone moved, that person was arrested and thrown in the camp's jail.

Not all camps were as strict as Chiang Kham. Some had bathrooms and hospitals. Some had garden plots. Some allowed trade between the Thai and Hmong. One refugee recalled being allowed to leave camp with her father to go shopping at a local mall for clothes.

There were makeshift camps located near the border of Thailand. One was named Tabok. Usually, refugees stayed for a few weeks before moving on to a more permanent camp. Namphong, a former military training camp, was located further inland.

It became necessary for the camps to be surrounded by barbed wire, to keep the refugees safe from outsiders. The fences also kept the refugees in place. Dr. Xoua Thao recalled the camp where he and his family lived as having houses that were divided in sections. He estimated there must have been close to thirty or forty thousand people living in Namphong.

"I remember we ate in a tent. They would ring a bell and we knew it was time to eat," said Thao. "I was not hungry but I'm sure there were big families who didn't get enough to eat. People lined up for everything—food, water."

Eventually all the camps were consolidated into one, Ban Vanai. People would live there for a long time—as long as ten years. The camp was primarily for people who wanted to wait to see if they could get back to Laos when things settled down.

Thao recalled life in the camp as boring and crowded:

"There was no privacy, everyone slept together with everyone else. Everyone's parents were depressed and scared. We [children] tried to keep busy by playing ball. Every day was the same. We just waited and waited to leave."

Thao's mother and other Hmong women would pass time by sewing *paj ntaub* Hmong embroidery which are colorful story blankets. In some cases, missionaries in the camp helped find a way for the women to get paid for their handiwork. But it was not very much money.

Even when they had money, there weren't enough supplies or food to buy. Men would help by sketching out picture-stories of life in Laos and their harrowing escapes. These scenes would be embroidered on cloth.

Thao said the men played the *qeej* bamboo pipes.
They were very depressed because they had been completely displaced. The men were more deeply affected by
the confinement than the women, who kept busy mind-
ing the children and preparing meals. The fact that their
wives now made money with embroidery depressed the
men even more. Most felt completely useless.

—Design Motif from a flower cloth by Thao Kons

Eventually, classes in English were offered, and some of the children decided to go to school while in the camps. Missionaries tried to help out by preparing the refugees for what to expect when they finally arrived in the United States. They taught English and basic skills, such as how to cross a street, what street signs meant, how to spend money and how to buy food, a completely new concept for people used to growing their own. The missionaries talked about how to be careful and watch out for thieves and told the refugees they would be targets for people who would try to take advantage of them.

In order to relocate to the United States, the refugees had to apply for sponsors. When Thao's family was told they had sponsors from the International Institute in Rhode Island, he was excited.

"Even though I didn't speak one single word of English and I had absolutely no idea of where we were going, I felt excited. Anything had to be better than this. But you had no control of your destiny. You just applied for sponsorship and hoped you got chosen. That's how my sister and her husband ended up in Georgia. They would split families [apart] if the sponsor needed to," said Thao.

Relocation disrupted the tight clan system of the Hmong that was the social support of hill tribes. When many Hmong families arrived in the United States, they found themselves spread out in different cities. As a result, a second migration occurred in the 1980s, as families began to move together again.

CHAPTER 7: Dr. Xoua Thao, First Hmong Medical Doctor

I am probably a priest, teacher, social worker, and then the physician part is very, very minimal other than writing prescriptions and making a diagnosis. So I see my profession or at least myself as a tool to solve problems, with family being the focus.—Dr. Xoua Thao

Young Xoua Thao looked out the window of the plane as he left the refugee camp in Thailand. Below him he saw, for the last time, mountains dotted with cone-shaped trees, deep green jungles and great rivers running into the South China Sea. He was on his way to the United States.

He didn't know it at the time, but he was to become a Hmong pioneer in education, medicine, social service and law. Dr. Xoua Thao, the founder of the Xoua Thao Medical Center in Saint Paul, Minnesota, has become an inspiration to Hmong people by serving and building his community. He is a Western-trained medical practitioner who constantly straddles two very different cultures and keeps both worlds in balance.

Thao's story begins as a young boy growing up in a worn-torn country. His quiet, rural life was completely turned upside down when his family began to live as fugitives. Thao's amazing story illustrates the tremendous capacity of the human heart to forgive, to let go of the past and to begin again.

The village Thao was born in was called Xam Luam. It was located about 120 miles north of Laos' capital city, Vientiane. People lived an agrarian (farming) life and community life was very well organized.

"Before the war came, we didn't have to move the entire family when we needed to move to new farmland. Sometimes we could stay in one place for many years, walking to the new farm. We moved only when the land was too far away from the village to walk to and from," said Thao. That meant that the farms and the fields were sometimes miles away from the village.

Dr. Xoua Thao

—Physician

Crops on the Thao family's farm included melons, yams, beans, sugar cane and corn. The family grew its own rice, which was a staple of the Hmong diet. Although they were surrounded by a jungle, Thao says the family didn't often forage for fruits or roots. For one thing, it was dangerous because of the tigers and other wild animals.

"One of the many things about Hmong life that is so rewarding is the fact that there is a celebration that acknowledges our indebtedness to all that has gone before us," said Thao. "Nothing is ever taken for granted. Aside from the births, weddings, funerals, and the New Year, there are other opportunities to give offerings like when we plant and harvest the fields or when we move to a new village."

Looking back, Thao said he sees his journey as a great adventure, because he was so young. He could tell, however, that his older brothers and his parents were worried about getting out of Laos safely.

"We would have to walk so many hours every day that we ended up leaving a lot of things behind each time. During our last move, when we crossed the Mekong River, we had nothing left except the clothes on our backs and maybe a few silver bars."

The Thaos—fifteen of them, including in-laws—were met by Thai people who took them to a street where they were picked up by a truck and brought to the initial camp named Tabok. They stayed for a couple of weeks, then were transferred to a big camp called Namphong.

That camp is where Thao got his first glimpse of street lights. From that moment on, he was taken up by the excitement of what might lie ahead. He had a good feeling about his future and knew that this would be one of many firsts in his life.

"In the camps a story was circulating that America was the land of dragons. So you can't drop anything because the dragon will get it. When I got off the airplane I said, Oh my! There is so much land there must be a lot of dragons."

Even with the dragons awaiting, Thao found the idea

of going to America really exciting. He looked forward to living there. But he also had a sad feeling that he might not see home again. By the time the family arrived in Providence, Rhode Island, they had come nine thousand miles from Laos.

The Thao children came to the United States first— followed by their parents, a month later. The trip was long and tiring.

"We flew from Bangkok to Hong Kong to Tokyo to San Francisco to Providence. We slept overnight in Hong Kong. It took us only about two days in a commercial plane to make the entire trip. Whole families would travel together on the plane, but once we got to San Francisco, people would start to split off," said Thao.

The family stayed in a hotel in Bangkok for medical examinations, which included asking about family history of disease and undergoing drug tests for opium use. The hotel was very exciting to Thao. He saw swimming pools, lights, music, restaurants, big beds with white sheets, bathrooms and showers.

"I was so surprised at what I saw when we went from the camps to the Bangkok Hotel. There were lights, pools, cars, and they even passed out towels for your face! I didn't know where or how to go to a bathroom so I held it in for 24 hours until I finally figured it out," said Thao. "When we got to San Francisco, there were a lot of other surprises. Looking out the windows and seeing other people outside, some of the older folks would walk right into the window. They would get big bumps on their heads."

About his trip, Thao said that "we were the second wave of Hmong families to come to Providence. It was April, 1976. Our sponsors put us on the second floor of a house that was already occupied by a Hmong family that had got there ahead of us. I remember me and my two brothers tried to sleep there but we couldn't. It was too cold. There were no windows and no heat and they put us on army cots and we could not sleep there, because it was so cold. Boy, that was a shock. It was cold. Back home, the coldest month was December and there might be a little frost on the ground. But never snow."

Thao was dedicated to learning and embraced his studies with enthusiasm: "I put my heart and soul into learning English. I studied very hard with five hours a day in an English as a Second Language (ESL) class, plus I attended night classes"

Since Thao was a boy, he was allowed to leave the farm to go to school in Laos. He learned to read in Lao and French and excelled in arithmetic. That was exceptional, since the illiteracy rate in certain regions of Laos was 99 percent. Thao said the school had all kids mixed together. It wasn't unusual to see a 14-year-old sitting next to a 6-year-old in the same class.

"In the United States, I didn't start school right away; it took me a whole month to get the physical and the shots (immunizations). They put me in seventh grade for two weeks, then school was over for the summer. When fall came, I had learned enough English that I thought I could skip eighth grade, so I went back to the same school and asked to be in ninth. If I was in Laos, I'd be in ninth grade because I had math skills equivalent to those of the ninth grade here in America," said Thao. "They let me try it, and it was hard. But after that year, I did very well in school—mostly A's."

Thao accomplished his goals by being disciplined. He had learned structure as part of his life back in Laos. Rather than falling back on his inability to speak English or his refugee status to get by, Thao decided to keep structure in his life and use it to his advantage. He would come home from school, have a bowl of noodles, play a little soccer and then hit the books. During his high school years, Thao never saw a movie, went to a party or hung out at the mall.

School was not an easy time for Thao. He was treated poorly by his classmates. Sometimes they spit on his food and called him names. Other times, classmates would rub his head and run. This was considered a very bad thing for the Hmong, since they believe that the soul can escape from the tops of their heads.

"The other kids would rub my hair, spit on my lunch and call me Chink! I didn't know what that meant until later," recalled Thao. "I went to Central High School in Providence, which was a big place. Boy, was I shocked everyone was so rowdy and rude."

Cultural differences became apparent at this point in Thao's life. Up until then, he had lived with other Hmong his whole life, even in the new house in Providence. The Hmong of Laos rarely intermingled with other cultures, unlike in America which is known as a "melting pot" of cultures.

American kids are raised to be independent and outgoing. They learn at an early age to speak their minds and are encouraged to find their own identities and express them. On the other hand, Hmong kids are raised to be part of a bigger family. It didn't take long for Hmong kids to seek each other out for moral support in this new country.

"We were very quiet. I didn't understand when the other kids would call me "dude." What was that? There were five or six of us Hmong at that school and we hung around together all the time and were very supportive of each other. We ate together everyday."

Looking back, Thao says he sometimes thinks it was a good thing he didn't understand all the things his classmates were saying to him.

Thao graduated from high school sixth in his class of 254, even though he had spoken no English four years before he enrolled. While he was in high school, he started to think about college and what he wanted to do with his education.

Thao was sick as a child. As a result, he grew up close to his brother-in-law, who was a medic in the village, the only person who had pills, vitamins and bandages. Thao said that experience, and his parents' work as healers, helped him decide to become a doctor. He also was deeply influenced by his three-week hospitalization in Providence when he first arrived.

"I was exposed to the medical institutions in both Laos

and here in America. I became more and more interested in becoming a doctor, so I studied my sciences and math hard and started applying to medical schools."

In 1984, Thao graduated with a B.A. in Biology from Brown University and went on to the Brown-Dartmouth program in medicine, where he received his medical degree in 1989. While finishing his medical education, he enrolled in the Harvard University School of Public Health. He got his Master's Degree in Public Health that same year.

Thao said that the education to become a doctor was difficult, but nothing compared to running his own clinic with his own patients. His largely Hmong practice was started in Saint Paul, Minnesota, in August, 1995. His decision to move to the area was made because his brothers and sisters were already there.

In the medical arts, cultural differences between Western and Hmong traditions are more pronounced. In Laos, when a person became ill, it was believed to be because the spirits were angry or had escaped, or ancestors were trying to send a message. The person would then visit a shaman or spiritual healer.

In America, when a person becomes ill, it is believed there is something clinically wrong with him or her. Healing the body is the basis of Western medicine. Healing the mind and soul is the basis of Eastern medicine.

"I grew up with shamanism. This was all that I knew, so when I went to medical school, I was surprised to find out how little the spiritual aspect of healing was talked about," said Thao.

The medical school used cadavers (dead persons) for teaching. Thao grew up with the idea that people would be reincarnated, so a person would never cut up a dead body. He felt a lot of personal hesitation when asked to do that. He recognizes it was hard for all students but it was especially hard for him.

For Thao, the hardest part of being a medical doctor is getting his patients to understand the concept of prevention. His older patients have the most difficulty.

He frequently sees patients who come in and want whatever is ailing them cured on the spot. It is difficult for him to explain that there are certain steps the doctor takes in treating an illness.

"Opium was the best cure the older ones knew of in the old country. You would lie down, smoke some, and go to sleep. Lots of times, when you woke up the pain would be gone, at least for a little while. I can't do that here and I have to tell them that it is illegal."

But Thao respects his patients' beliefs and allows them to use the best of both worlds, provided it doesn't involve anything illegal. As a doctor, he knows it is important for his patients to have a sense of well-being, and if that means they want to see a shaman, then that is fine.

"I have to read my patients' minds. I need to know that they are thinking of life after death and how they are going to come back in the next life. When my terminal patients reject treatments like chemotherapy, I respect that. I tell them they may need pain medication and we try that route. When I know they are afraid to face dying, I use the analogy of the sun. That we all will set someday. But I like to stretch it as long as I can to give them a few more hours. Some people choose not to do anything and let the sun set in its course. And those I respect."

For health care workers, it is especially vital to understand the importance of the shaman in the Hmong culture. Since the shaman was consulted for nearly every medical problem in Laos, it is sometimes confusing to understand Western medical practices. Thao said he doesn't mind when his patients visit shamans, as long as they do it in conjunction with a prescribed course of action.

Thao explained that a shaman must go into a trance and communicate directly with the *dab* (spirits) to find out why the person is sick. This involves riding the spirit of a horse that takes him all over the world seeking answers. The shaman, traditionally a man, sits at his altar and bounces up and down for hours at a time as he takes his spiritual ride.

In addition, the family of the sick person must offer

sacrifices to the spirits. They burn paper that resembles money so that it will go up to the ancestor's spirit who will take it in exchange for the patient's spirit. They sacrifice a pig or chicken and cook it, inviting the ancestor to join in the feast.

Success of the shaman does not always mean the disease is cured. Success is measured by whether the life-soul is properly shown the way.

Thao's accomplishments don't end with his medical practice. He has gone back to school and received his law degree. His wife is an attorney.

"My dream is not to be a doctor forever. I want to pull all the Hmong people together. My next phase of my life is to travel to Hmong communities all over the world—China, Thailand, Vietnam, Argentina, France, French Guyana, Canada. I want to create a sense that we are still a people without land. A nation without borders."

CHAPTER 8: Ying Vang, First Hmong Catholic Priest in the United States

My belief in God made it easier for me to be in America. It made it a much less scary place to be.—Father Ying Vang.

Shamanistic animism was the spiritual backbone of the Hmong culture. In Laos, it was a way for people to communicate with their ancestors—to ask them for guidance and protection. Shamanism was also a health system which made it more deeply entrenched in Hmong life than if it were only a religion.

The Hmong worshiped many gods. A story is told about a very special god, *Dab Phuaj Thaub*, who lived on a mountain in Laos. This god was given sacrifices and, in turn, it ensured the well-being of the tribe by granting productive harvests. When the Americans came during the war, they turned the mountain top into a landing strip for airplanes. The god was wiped out by the dynamite blasts. This meant the Hmong were no longer protected and assured good fortune.

Since most Hmong refugees were sponsored by Christian organizations, many Hmong converted to Christianity in America. This was seen by some of the elders as the worst thing that could happen to their culture since the bombing in Laos. To them, to believe in shamanism is the very definition of being Hmong.

Anxiety and mixed feelings about Christianity have pervaded Hmong culture in America. In some instances, when only one partner in a marriage becomes Christian, the result is divorce. In other instances, arguments over religion cause families to break up. To keep peace, some Hmong combine both Christianity and Shamanism.

When Ying Vang, the first Hmong Catholic Priest in the United States was ordained, the celebration included traditional Hmong blessings. Strings were tied around his wrists to wish him good luck.

For Vang, it was the war that showed him what real human suffering was about. The 13 year-old orphan began to dream of being a priest in order to help others. He realized that in order to be happy, he would have to make that dream come true.

Vang's life has been far from easy. After escaping Laos, he endured five years in a Thailand refugee camp, where he learned his parents and other relatives had been killed by communist soldiers. Comforted by Catholic missionaries, he abandoned spirit worship and converted to Catholicism.

In an interview with the *Fresno Bee*, Vang said of the Hmong who still worship spirits: "I try to see them in the eyes of God. They're people like me and God loves everyone."

Vang was born in 1963, the sixth of nine children. His family were farmers in northeastern Laos. Like many other Hmong, his family was caught up in the war and wanted to escape the communists. There wasn't enough money for all of them to go, so his parents went back into the mountains to farm. Twelve-year-old Vang, his two older brothers and two cousins set out for the Mekong River. Traveling by car, boat, and foot they reached the Thai border and sneaked across. They wound up in a refugee camp with about thirty thousand other Hmong. Vang lived in the camp for five years.

He later learned that his parents and two sisters had been killed. They were caught fleeing Laos and were murdered. Vang came to the U.S. in 1980, sponsored by a Catholic church in Rochester, Minnesota. He went to Rochester Lourdes High School knowing very little English. According to Vang, it was his faith in God that made the new world a less strange place.

He graduated at twenty-one and enrolled in Crosier Seminary in Onamia, Minnesota, where he received his two-year degree. He then transferred to Immaculate Heart of Mary Seminary in Winona, Minnesota, where he began studies for the priesthood.

Vang has managed to keep both Hmong and American identities. While his siblings support his priesthood, they are concerned about his vow of celibacy and how he will not have a family of his own.

Vang realizes how difficult it is for Hmong Christians who feel they are compromising their faith if they attend traditional Hmong ceremonies. He knows of several who still respectfully honor their past by attending Hmong celebrations, but do not participate in Hmong spirit worship.

Vang stays in touch with a Hmong priest in Laos and hopes to return there some day.

CHAPTER 9: Choua Lee, First Elected Hmong Official in the United States

The culture shock and not knowing the language was overwhelming but eventually we learned English. We used to watch television cartoons to learn. We loved Star Trek because Captain Kirk and his crew survived alien cultures, like we were doing.—Choua Lee.

Traditional Hmong culture treated woman as inferior persons. They were objects that were owned first by their families and then by their husbands. Women walked behind their husbands, usually five paces back. They had no legal status, so they could not negotiate contracts or sign documents. They had no say as to whom they would marry. Once a partner was chosen, a "bride price" (or dowry) would be negotiated among the males of both families.

Divorce was allowed in the Hmong culture, but the woman could never initiate it. The usual outcome of a divorce meant the wife ended up with nothing: no home, no children, no family. Education was almost always restricted to males.

Given that women weren't even permitted to vote in the Hmong culture, it was amazing that Choua Lee became the first Hmong elected to public office in the United States. Lee said she never even expected to be endorsed by the DFL (Democratic Farmer's League) in the first place. Yet after only one ballot, 62% of the delegates voted for her. In the general election in November 1991, she surprised herself again by being the top vote-getter in the election for one of the four open seats on the St. Paul School Board.

Lee doesn't talk much about her accomplishment as a woman. She sometimes thinks the bigger accomplishment is finding her way around the city where her family had settled.

"It got so confusing. At first, I couldn't tell the difference between the inside of a plane and the inside of an building," said Lee. "But once I figured out that part, I had a hard time telling streets apart. All the buildings looked same. It was confusing."

Lee recalls her first day in an elementary school in Chicago. She was seven years old, and unable to speak English. Everything about the new school was different from the one in Long Cheng, Laos. The Hmong school was a hut in open field. The school in the United States was many stories high, with such new and strange inventions as desks, chalkboards and flush toilets. Back home, she could understand what the teachers were saying. In the new school, all she could do was watch and wonder what was going on.

"I can remember getting lost when it came time for me to go home. It was raining and all I could think about was how much all the buildings looked the same," Lee remembered. "Even when a girl from class came to help me, I didn't know what she was saying."

Eventually, her parents and the principal found Lee and brought her home, but she will never forget that feeling of being completely lost. It was from that understanding that Lee vowed to help close the language gap between the parents, teachers, and student.

"I want to be there for the Hmong. I want to help people get out of survival mode and into the system. Education is the only way for that to happen," said Lee.

During her tenure as a school board member, Lee found it difficult to adapt to the American style of politics. It was customary for Hmong to expect their leaders to stand alone as they represented them. In the United States, politics is more of a group effort—following the leader.

In Laos, Lee lived in Long Cheng with her parents who employed people to tend their livestock and farm the 300 acres they owned. While not rich, her family was considered to be better off than most.

The family also had a sewing shop that Lee's mother managed. Her father was a commander in the Laotian army. Their house was large enough to house thirty or forty soldiers at a time.

When Laos fell to communism in 1975, the family had

to flee their farm and business.

"We didn't want any communist coming in and taking what had, so we butchered all our livestock, one right after the other," Lee remembered.

Within ten days of the news that the communists had won the war, Lee says the family took what they could carry and started off for the capitol of Laos, Vientiane. Lee's father was especially worried for his life, since he held a position in the army. In fact, her father dressed in woman's clothes so he wouldn't be recognized.

"I remember hiding along the way. There were checkpoints where communist soldiers would check to see if we had any military officials with us. If they found any, they were sent to labor camps, or worse," said Lee.

Once her family got to the capital, they got on a crowded boat that took them across the Mekong River to Thailand. They were forced to camp out and live off the land until they found a way to get to the United States.

Fortunately for Lee, her parents were supportive.

"My parents didn't have any sons, so they tended to treat me like one. I think that gave me an advantage. They told me I could do anything a man could do and really emphasized getting an education," Lee recalled.

Lee served one term on the St. Paul School Board and chose not to seek reelection, but instead devote her time to her family and business pursuits.

CHAPTER 10: Rev. Bea Vue-Benson, First Hmong Woman Lutheran Minister

Hmong confuse Christianity with culture. They believe if you become a Christian, everything has to be new. They see the Hmong way as the old way.—Reverend Bea Vue-Benson.

The communists, or "red ants" as the Hmong called them, were coming closer each day. Cher Xiong Vue and his family were living in a mountain cave when he decided it was time to move on to Bouam Long. Before they started the journey, he made an offer to the spirits to ensure them safe passage.

Bea Vue remembers that day when her dad, a shaman, laid out offerings at the altar. Incense, rice and bamboo were part of the ceremony. He called upon the spirits of his mother and father and promised them silver bars and pork if they would guide them through this ordeal.

Like nearly every other Hmong refugee, Vue-Benson's life had been touched and scarred by the Vietnam War. The highlands of Laos where they lived were of strategic importance in the early 1960s, because the Ho Chi Minh trail ran through them. The trail was the North Vietnamese army's main supply line linking North and South Vietnam. The CIA thought the Hmong could disrupt the supply line, so it trained farmers to be soldiers. Vue-Benson's father, Cher Xiong Vue, was among them. He was on guard duty in 1971 when a bomb exploded near his post and killed him.

To escape from the advancing communists, his widow took the family on a perilous journey through Laos and across the Mekong River into Thailand. They spent almost three years in a crowded refugee camp in Thailand. Vue-Benson's main recollection of being nine years old is the hard work in the camp.

"I remember doing hard labor for the Thai farmers," she said. "We didn't have any income so we'd work for them digging potatoes or roots. We had to carry our own firewood and I had to go into the woods to collect it. We

Reverend Bea Vue-Benson

—Luthern Minister

also had to carry our own water. There would be really long lines and I remember having to start the fire first thing in the morning," said Vue-Benson.

In 1978, the Trinity Lutheran Church of Eau Claire, Wisconsin, sponsored the Vue family's entry into the United States.

Despite strong Hmong customs concerning women, Vue Benson decided to go to college instead of becoming a wife at an early age. She attended St. Olaf College in Northfield, Minnesota. Vue was also seeing a man her family didn't like. To put an end to it, they arranged a marriage for her to a Hmong man she hardly knew. Vue-Benson said she ran away from him eight times.

Finally, after striking a deal between the two families, she was able to leave the marriage and resume school in Northfield. She had started out as a nursing major, but her experience with marriage prompted her to switch to women's studies and religion.

She enrolled at Luther Northwestern Theological Seminary in St. Paul, Minnesota in 1990, where she trained to become a Lutheran minister.

In an interview, Bea Vue-Benson said most Hmong struggle to become Christian without giving up cultural traditions and family. With about 40 percent of the Hmong population converting to Christianity, many Hmong merge the two worlds by attending family feasts without worshiping spirits.

Hmong confuse Christianity with culture, Vue-Benson said.

"They believe if you become a Christian, everything has to be new. They see the Hmong way as the old way," said Vue-Benson. "But I would like to see Christian worship services include more of the Hmong practices."

CHAPTER 11: Christopher Thao, First Hmong Attorney in the United States

Although life in America affords more opportunities, adjusting is often a one-way street.—Christopher Thao.

Christopher Thao said it is hard for Hmong refugees to adapt to new laws and customs in the United Sates. They do not trust the system because they do not understand it. To illustrate his point, he tells a story:

"A judge is about to decide a case that involves a Southeast Asian refugee. The refugee stands up and tells the judge that he and the opponent in the case should drink a magic potion. Then the judge would know where to place the blame. The refugee believes the liquid would be needed to bring justice to light because back in Laos, the potion would kill the person who was guilty within one year. Knowing about impending death if they lie, the person who was willing to drink it was deemed the truthful one.

"In our homeland, the Lao police and government are generally corrupt and harsh," Thao said. "If you were arrested in Laos for anything and put in jail, chances are slim you would ever get out. However, we didn't have jails in our Hmong villages."

Imprisonment wasn't practiced. Instead, various forms of public humiliation were used. Losing face was considered a fate worse than death. After a thief paid back what he stole, he was paraded through the village with his hands tied, while the villagers jeered.

"This system worked because it helped the criminal become a better person by living through the shame and it kept a primary provider with his family," said Thao. "There were different punishments for different crimes. Sometimes a public apology was needed and other times the potion was used."

While in the camps, Christopher Thao dreamed of coming to the United States to get an education. When he was 18 years old, he was assigned a sponsor family who lived

Christopher Thao

—Lawyer

near Jasper, Arkansas. When he arrived at the small town in the Ozarks, he realized that he was the only Asian person within a thirty-mile radius.

"I lived with a very nice elderly couple who had no children in a mobile home," said Thao. "I was so lonely and wanted to be with other Hmong people so I called my caseworker in New York and told them I just can't survive like this. I asked them for bus fare to Pennsylvania, where some of my cousins had settled."

Thao remembers that his sponsors were upset that he wanted to leave. After he told them how much he needed to be with his own family, they drove him to the bus station.

"All I had was a bus ticket," said Thao. "I didn't have any money and my sponsors weren't going to give me any. I thought about what to do and decided to make a collect call to an American missionary I met once in Laos."

Proving his resourcefulness and determination, Thao got the missionary to call someone in Jasper to bring him ten dollars.

After a twenty-five hour trip on the bus to Philadelphia, Thao had another hurdle to clear. The church that had sponsored his relatives refused to help him, because he had left his original sponsors. He called his caseworker in New York again, who paid for his bus fare to a resort in the Pocono Mountains, where he became a janitor.

"While I was working as a janitor, I found out there was a college nearby," said Thao. "So I went to the East Stroudsburg State College and talked them into letting me enroll as a temporary, non-degree student."

After a year, Thao became a regular student. With the help of special refugee programs and student loans, he stayed on for two years.

After his parents and the rest of his siblings arrived in the Philadelphia area, he transferred to West Chester State College to be close to them. He also took a year off school to work as a refugee caseworker in order to help support his family.

Another major event interrupted his education in 1980. His parents decided they wanted to move to Minnesota to be near other friends and relatives, so Thao moved the group in his car to the Twin Cities of Minneapolis and St. Paul. In order to help his family settle in, Thao took a job writing lesson plans for the Minneapolis Public Schools and managed to finish his degree at Hamline University in St. Paul.

When Thao found out his dad was terminally ill, he enrolled in William Mitchell College of Law. After two-and-a-half years, Thao's dad got his dying wish—to see his son graduate with a law degree. His father died a month later.

Even though Thao was in America, he still held his Hmong values close to heart. He had demonstrated his commitment to Hmong tradition several times. However, in 1981, Thao took another step to please his father, by getting married.

"My father told me he wasn't sure when was going to die but he knew he was sick," said Thao. "He didn't want to die knowing I was still a bachelor."

Thao took immediate action by calling his cousins and asking them if they knew of any beautiful girl he could marry. His cousins found a Hmong girl for him. He met her and they got to know each other for a month, then they got married. They are still married to this day and happily raising their children.

Thao readily acknowledges the marriage was based on an obligation and promise he made to his father. He is quick to add that it was a good decision because it worked out so well.

Thao is a licensed attorney who serves mostly the refugee and immigrant Asian populations in Minnesota. He still encounters conflicts between the "old and new." For Christopher Thao, his dream is a future where Hmong can hold on to their values and traditions while still becoming American.

AFTERWORD: Bridging Two Worlds

The first group of Hmong who came to America included parents and their children. It was the children that took advantage of the educational system and made impressive strides toward a new life

For the older Hmong, the successes were of a different nature. Learning to cross a street at the right moment and the right place was a big accomplishment. Learning to sign their name or a few words of English was a great challenge. Learning to drive a car meant regaining some of their former independence. Most of the older Hmong knew that it was their children who stood the best chance of success in America. Many elder Hmong will never consider themselves a part of both worlds.

It was the responsibility of the Hmong children to act as go-betweens for the generations. For some Hmong, it came down to picking and choosing practices from both worlds. Many of the first refugee children to arrive were old enough to remember the Hmong traditions and to keep up Hmong culture. They continue to practice social activities which result from having more than two generations living under one roof.

As Dr. Xoua Thao, says: "To us, having more than one generation under one roof is considered a household of harmony, strength and wealth. We have a community here in our household that will be continued with my sons when they grow up and marry."

If Thao were to have any daughters, they would leave the home to join their husbands' household.

Thao said there were so many differences in the two cultures that he felt it was very important for him to take what he had learned and pass it along to other Hmong.

"I sometimes feel it was us, the wave of the first younger immigrants, that are the most successful. We learned everything from scratch and learned it fast. We looked at this whole thing as a big opportunity. Education was there and success was there for our taking. I speak to students a lot. I tell them, if you feel an injustice, any discrimination, then you work on it. If you feel any racism in class, then you talk about it. You prepare yourself to be a contributing member of this society."

HMONG GLOSSARY

Choj—Silver bars used as currency by the Hmong in Laos.

Dab—Spirits.

Hmoob—Hmong.

Hu Plig—Soul-calling ceremony performed on the third day after the birth of a child.

Kab Ke Pam Tuag—"Showing the Way" funeral ritual.

Kher Kong—Ritual of chanting and using other symbols to cast spells or cure illnesses.

Khi Tes—Ritual of tying the wrists of the bride and groom with pieces of yarn for good luck.

Neng—A healing spirit that resides in and lives in the body of a shaman.

Niam—Mother

Not Tsiab Pebcaug—Referring to "eat the feast of the 30th" or Hmong New Year.

Paj Ntaub—Hmong stitched quilt, usually depicting a story. Sometimes called flower cloth.

Pov Pob—Ball-tossing game played among men during the New Year.

Qeej—A musical instrument made of bamboo pipes, played like a mouth organ.

Qeej Tu Siav—A funeral song played on the qeej, meaning "The Saddest Song."

Saub—A person who has special powers to heal and tell fortunes.

Sher Qeng—A string tied around the wrist or neck to ward off evil spirits.

Tshuaj Npua—A yellow rain which was a chemical weapon of the Vietnam war; its literal translation is "poison."

Tsho—Shirt, used to refer to a newborn's placenta or afterbirth.

Tus Npua Tsiab—The feast pig that is customarily slaughtered for the New Year celebration.

Tus Ntau Ntuas—The drum man during ceremonies.

Txiv—Father.

Txiv Neeb—Shaman.
Xeem—Clan system.

TO LEARN MORE: SOURCES

With the Hmong being among the more recent immigrants to the United States, there is not a great deal of printed material for the younger person to learn about the history, life and culture of the Hmong. As a result, to learn more about the Hmong, it can be rewarding to turn to the Internet, where the following web sites can provide useful information:

http://www.hmongnet.org offers the WWW Hmong Homepage. It is a comprehensive guide to the history and cultural life of the Hmong people as well as links to other web sites. You will find information about the Hmong people throughout the world as well as the United States.

http://www.homongstudies.org is a web site devoted to advanced scholarship about the Hmong people. While the studies, census reports, and newsletter are prepared for researchers, the links to other web sites and the scholarly Hmong bibliographies can identify useful information for the serious research project about the Hmong.

http://www.hmongcenter.org is the web site of the Hmong Cultural Center in Saint Paul, Minnesota. Its purpose is to promote personal development of the Hmong through cultural exhibits while also providing resources that enhance cultural understanding between the Hmong and other people. In so doing, the center provides a site with both museum and educational features and information about the Hmong and their cultural life. The center also has a current list of books about Laos and the Hmong and offers the books for sale along with examples of Hmong arts and crafts.

http://lib.uci.edu/rrsc/hmong.html provides information about textile art and the beautiful textiles of the Hmong. It is a web site maintained by the University of California–Irvine, where a research collection of Hmong textiles is located.

There are a number of periodical articles which have detailed many of the problems faced by the Hmong as they adapt to a new life in America, and these can be found in a number of the city and regional magazines published in the United States.

A periodical article of a more general nature, however, is the following:

Fadiman, Anne. Heroes' Welcome. Civilization, Volume 4, 53+ August/September 1997. This article, approximately ten pages in length, is illustrated with photographs of the Hmong.

Finally, there are two books which can supply information about the Hmong in the United States if you are up to the challenge.

The books are:

Faderman, Lillian. I Begin My Life All Over, The Hmong and the American Immigrant Experience, Beacon Press, 1998.

Fadiman, Anne. The Spirit Catches You and You Fall Down, A Hmong Child, Her American Doctors and the Collision of Two Cultures, Noonday Press, 1997.

Index